2. *Ea*... *Cookbook*
3. ***Easy Beans Cookbook***

Remember this box set is about **EASY** cooking.

In the ***Easy Sushi Cookbook*** you will learn the easiest methods to prepare almost every type of Japanese Sushi i.e. *California Rolls, the Perfect Sushi Rice, Crab Rolls, Osaka Style Sushi*, and so many others.

Then we go on to *Dump Dinners*. Nothing can be easier than a Dump Dinner. In the ***Easy Dump Dinner Cookbook*** we will learn how to master our slow cookers and make some amazingly unique dinners that will take almost ***no effort***.

Finally in the ***Easy Beans Cookbook*** we tackle one of my favorite side dishes: Beans. There are so many delicious ways to make Baked Beans and Bean Salads that I had to share them.

So stay till the end and then keep on cooking with my *Easy Specialty Cookbook Box Set*!

Stay To the End of the Cookbook and Receive....

I really appreciate when people, take the time to read all of my recipes.

So, as a gift for reading this entire cookbook you will receive a **massive collection of special recipes.**

Read to the end of and get my *Easy Specialty Cookbook Box Set for FREE*!

This box set includes the following:

1. *Easy Sushi Cookbook*

EASY CHILI COOKBOOK

THE EFFORTLESS CHEF SERIES

By
Chef Maggie Chow
Copyright © 2015 by Saxonberg
Associates
All rights reserved

Published by
BookSumo, a division of Saxonberg
Associates
http://www.booksumo.com/

ABOUT THE AUTHOR.

Maggie Chow is the author and creator of your favorite *Easy Cookbooks* and *The Effortless Chef Series*. Maggie is a lover of all things related to food. Maggie loves nothing more than finding new recipes, trying them out, and then making them her own, by adding or removing ingredients, tweaking cooking times, and anything to make the recipe not only taste better, but be easier to cook!

For a complete listing of all my books please see my author page.

Introduction

Welcome to *The Effortless Chef Series*! Thank you for taking the time to download the *Easy Chili Cookbook*. Come take a journey with me into the delights of easy cooking. The point of this cookbook and all my cookbooks is to exemplify the effortless nature of cooking simply.

In this book we focus on Chili. You will find that even though the recipes are simple, the taste of the dishes is quite amazing.

So will you join me in an adventure of simple cooking? If the answer is yes (and I hope it is) please consult the table of contents to find the dishes you are most interested in. Once you are ready jump right in and start cooking.

— Chef Maggie Chow

TABLE OF CONTENTS

STAY TO THE END OF THE COOKBOOK AND RECEIVE..2

About the Author. 5

Introduction 7

Table of Contents 8

Any Issues? Contact Me 12

Legal Notes 13

Common Abbreviations 14

Chapter 1: Easy Chili Recipes 15

    Chili I 15

    (Buffalo Meat) 15

    (Denver Style) 15

    Chili II 19

    (Chicken, Peppers, and Jalapenos) ..19

    Chili III 22

(Ancho Chili, Sausage, Beef, and Garlic) 22
Chili IV 26
(Chipotle) 26
Chili V 30
(Rustic) 30
Chili VI 33
(Turkey, Salsa, and Zucchini) 33
Chili VII 37
(3 Bean) 37
(Vegetarian Approved) 37
Chili VIII 41
(Cloves, Allspice, and Cinnamon) 41
(Ohio Style) 41
Chili IX 44
(Pork, Salsa, and Beans) 44
Chili X 47
(White Beans) 47
Chili XI 50
(Maggie's Easy Style) 50
Chili XII 53

(White Beans and Tomatillos) 53

Chili XIII...56

(Black Bean and Basil).....................56

Chili XIV 59

(White Beans and Turkey) 59

Chili XV 62

(Crock Pot I) 62

Chili XVI 65

(3 Bean II)..65

(Vegetarian Approved) 65

Chili XVII...68

(North Carolina Style).....................68

Chili XVIII 71

(Quinoa and Cilantro).....................71

Chili XIX..75

(Apricots and Raisins) 75

Chili XX 78

(Autumn) 78

Chili XXI..81

(Texas Style) 81

Chili XXII...85

(3 Pepper) 85

(Jalapenos, Habaneros, and Anaheim)
....85

Chili XXIII 89

(Cannellini and Cheddar) 89

Chili XXIV...92

(Roman Style)...................................92

Chili XXV 95

(Backroad Style) 95

THANKS FOR READING! NOW LET'S TRY
SOME **SUSHI** AND **DUMP DINNERS**.....98

Come On... 100

Let's Be Friends :) 100

Can I Ask A Favour?.........................101

Interested in Other Easy Cookbooks?
....102

ANY ISSUES? CONTACT ME

If you find that something important to you is missing from this book please contact me at maggie@booksumo.com.

I will try my best to re-publish a revised copy taking your feedback into consideration and let you know when the book has been revised with you in mind.

:)

— Chef Maggie Chow

LEGAL NOTES

ALL RIGHTS RESERVED. NO PART OF THIS BOOK MAY BE REPRODUCED OR TRANSMITTED IN ANY FORM OR BY ANY MEANS. PHOTOCOPYING, POSTING ONLINE, AND / OR DIGITAL COPYING IS STRICTLY PROHIBITED UNLESS WRITTEN PERMISSION IS GRANTED BY THE BOOK'S PUBLISHING COMPANY. LIMITED USE OF THE BOOK'S TEXT IS PERMITTED FOR USE IN REVIEWS WRITTEN FOR THE PUBLIC AND/OR PUBLIC DOMAIN.

Common Abbreviations

cup(s)	C.
tablespoon	tbsp
teaspoon	tsp
ounce	oz.
pound	lb

*All units used are standard American measurements

Chapter 1: Easy Chili Recipes

Chili I

(Buffalo Meat)

(Denver Style)

Ingredients

- 1 lb ground buffalo
- 1/2 tsp ground cumin
- 1 pinch cayenne pepper, or to taste
- 1 (10 oz.) can diced tomatoes with green chilis
- 1 (10.75 oz.) can tomato soup
- 1 (14.5 oz.) can kidney beans, drained
- 1 (15 oz.) can chili beans, drained
- 1/2 medium onion, diced
- 1/2 tsp minced garlic

- 1 Anaheim chili pepper, diced
- 1 poblano chili pepper, diced
- 2 tbsps chili powder
- 1 tsp red pepper flakes
- 1 1/2 tsps ground cumin
- 1/2 tsp cayenne pepper
- salt and ground black pepper to taste

Directions

- Get a bowl, mix: a bit of cayenne, half a tsp cumin, and the buffalo meat.
- Now stir fry your meat in some oil until browned all over. Then remove any excess oil. Put everything in your slow cooker.
- Add to the meat the following in the crock pot: black pepper, tomatoes and chilies, salt, tomato soup, half tsp cayenne, chili and kidney beans, 1.5 tsps cumin, onions, pepper flakes, garlic, chili powder, poblanos and Anaheim chilies.

- Place a lid on your slow cooker and set the heat to low for 8 hrs.
- Enjoy.

Amount per serving (6 total)

Timing Information:

Preparation	30 m
Cooking	8 h 10 m
Total Time	8 h 40 m

Nutritional Information:

Calories	219 kcal
Fat	2.8 g
Carbohydrates	29.8g
Protein	22.3 g
Cholesterol	39 mg
Sodium	725 mg

* Percent Daily Values are based on a 2,000 calorie diet.

Chili II

(Chicken, Peppers, and Jalapenos)

Ingredients

- 2 (10 oz.) cans chunk chicken, undrained
- 2 (16 oz.) cans chili beans, drained
- 3 (14.5 oz.) cans Mexican-style stewed tomatoes
- 1 (12 oz.) jar sliced jalapeno peppers
- 1 large onion, diced
- 2 large green bell peppers, seeded and diced
- 1 1/2 tbsps chili powder
- 2 tbsps ground cumin
- 10 C. water, or as needed
- 1 (14.5 oz.) can chicken broth
- salt to taste

Directions

- Get a big saucepan and add in: broth, chicken, cumin, beans, chili powder, tomatoes, bell peppers, jalapenos, and onions. Add in your water as well then get everything boiling.
- Once the mix is boiling set the heat to a medium level and let the contents gently boil for at least 65 mins.
- Add in your preferred amount of additional pepper and salt.
- Enjoy.

Amount per serving (15 total)

Timing Information:

Preparation	30 m
Cooking	1 h 15 m
Total Time	1 h 45 m

Nutritional Information:

Calories	149 kcal
Fat	4 g
Carbohydrates	18.8g
Protein	12.7 g
Cholesterol	23 mg
Sodium	714 mg

* Percent Daily Values are based on a 2,000 calorie diet.

Chili III

(Ancho Chili, Sausage, Beef, and Garlic)

Ingredients

- 10 dried ancho chilis - diced, stemmed and seeded
- 1/2 C. water
- 1/4 C. white wine vinegar
- 3 lbs hot Italian sausage, casings removed
- 3 lbs ground beef
- 1 white onion, diced
- 1 red onion, diced
- 1 sweet onion, diced
- 1 C. diced celery
- 1 C. diced carrots
- 10 cloves garlic, sliced
- 1 tsp salt
- 1 tsp black pepper
- 1 (6 oz.) can tomato paste
- 1 C. dry red wine

- 4 (14.5 oz.) cans diced tomatoes
- 1/4 C. Worcestershire sauce
- 1/4 C. hot pepper sauce
- 1 tbsp chili powder
- 2 tsps ground cumin
- 1 tbsp diced fresh parsley
- 1/2 C. honey
- 1 (16 oz.) can kidney beans, drained
- 1 (16 oz.) can pinto beans, drained

Directions

- Submerge your chilies in some vinegar and water for 35 mins then blend them until paste like for about 6 mins. Now place them in a bowl to the side.
- Begin to stir fry your beef and sausage until brown then place the meat to the side as well.
- Get a big pot and take 5 tbsps of the excess oils from the meat and

stir fry the following in it: garlic, onions, carrots, and celery.
- Cook the mix until the onions become see through.
- Now add some pepper and salt and the tomato paste, continue cooking until the onions caramelize.
- Now combine in the wine and scrape the pan. Add in: chili powder, hot sauce, cumin, meat, parsley, Worcestershire, and tomatoes.
- Get your chili boiling then add in your beans, honey, and pureed chilies.
- Get everything boiling again and place a lid on the pot.
- Reduce your heat to a gentle boil and cook for at least 3 hours.
- Enjoy.

Amount per serving (12 total)

Timing Information:

Preparation	1 h
Cooking	3 h 30 m
Total Time	4 h 30 m

Nutritional Information:

Calories	977 kcal
Fat	67.7 g
Carbohydrates	145.4g
Protein	43.2 g
Cholesterol	183 mg
Sodium	1735 mg

* Percent Daily Values are based on a 2,000 calorie diet.

Chili IV

(Chipotle)

Ingredients

- 2 lbs lean ground beef
- 1 onion, diced
- 2 red bell peppers, seeded and diced
- 2 jalapeno peppers, seeded and diced
- 4 cloves garlic, minced
- 1/2 C. chili powder
- 1/4 C. ground cumin
- 1 tsp salt
- 1 tsp ground black pepper
- 1 (6 oz.) can tomato paste
- 4 (15 oz.) cans kidney beans with liquid
- 1 (14.5 oz.) can Italian-style stewed tomatoes
- 1 (7 oz.) can chipotle peppers in adobo sauce
- 1 quart water, divided

- 1/4 C. all-purpose flour
- 1 tbsp rice vinegar

Directions

- Blend your adobo chilies until paste like for about 3 to 5 mins. Then place them to the side.
- Get a bowl, mix until smooth: 1 C. of water, and flour.
- Stir fry your beef until fully done then add in: chili powder, beans, jalapenos, tomato paste, cumin, onions, salt, garlic, pepper, and bell pepper.
- Stir and cook this mix for about 3 mins, and then add in the puree and also water (3 C.).
- Cook everything for 2 mins before adding the flour and the water mix. Stir everything before adding the vinegar.
- Get the mix boiling and then reduce the heat to a gentle simmering. Let the chili cook for 50 mins.

- Enjoy.

Amount per serving (16 total)

Timing Information:

Preparation	20 m
Cooking	1 h
Total Time	1 h 20 m

Nutritional Information:

Calories	295 kcal
Fat	13.5 g
Carbohydrates	27.1g
Protein	17.6 g
Cholesterol	43 mg
Sodium	649 mg

* Percent Daily Values are based on a 2,000 calorie diet.

Chili V

(Rustic)

Ingredients

- 4 skinless, boneless chicken breast halves
- 1 (16 oz.) jar salsa
- 2 tsps garlic powder
- 1 tsp ground cumin
- 1 tsp chili powder
- salt to taste
- ground black pepper to taste
- 1 (11 oz.) can Mexican-style corn
- 1 (15 oz.) can pinto beans

Directions

- Get a bowl, mix: chicken, pepper, garlic powder, salt, chili powder, and cumin.

- Now cook your salsa and chicken for 7 hours with a low heat in the slow cooker.
- After the meat has cooked for 4 hours take it out of the slow cooker and shred it.
- Place it back in the crock pot along with the beans and corn and continue cooking.
- Enjoy.

Amount per serving (6 total)

Timing Information:

Preparation	15 m
Cooking	12 h
Total Time	12 h 15 m

Nutritional Information:

Calories	188 kcal
Fat	2.3 g
Carbohydrates	22.6g
Protein	20.4 g
Cholesterol	41 mg
Sodium	1012 mg

* Percent Daily Values are based on a 2,000 calorie diet.

Chili VI

(Turkey, Salsa, and Zucchini)

Ingredients

- 3 tbsps vegetable oil, divided
- 1 1/2 lbs ground turkey
- 1 (1 oz.) package taco seasoning mix
- 1 tsp ground coriander
- 1 tsp dried oregano
- 1 tsp chili pepper flakes
- 2 tbsps tomato paste
- 1 (14.5 oz.) can beef broth
- 1 (7 oz.) can salsa
- 1 (14.5 oz.) can crushed tomatoes, or coarsely diced tomatoes packed in puree
- 1 (7 oz.) can diced green chili peppers
- 1 medium onion, finely diced
- 1 green bell pepper, diced

- 3 medium zucchini, halved lengthwise and sliced
- 1 bunch green onions, diced
- 1 C. sour cream
- 1 C. shredded Cheddar cheese

Directions

- Stir fry your turkey in oil after adding the following to it first: tomato paste, taco seasoning, chili flakes, coriander, and oregano.
- Cook the turkey until you have browned it and then add in the broth and boil the contents for 7 mins.
- Now add: green chilies, tomatoes, and salsa.
- Meanwhile in a separate pan stir fry: bell peppers, and onions for 6 mins then combine it with the chili.
- Reduce the heat on the chili to low level and gently boil everything.

- Now, stir fry for 6 mins, your zucchini in oil, then pour it in with the chili.
- Cook the chili for about 17 more mins and add some water if you find that it is too thick for your liking.
- When serving your chili add the following to each serving: cheddar, green onions, and a dollop of sour cream.
- Enjoy.

Amount per serving (6 total)

Timing Information:

Preparation	15 m
Cooking	55 m
Total Time	1 h 10 m

Nutritional Information:

Calories	506 kcal
Fat	31.9 g
Carbohydrates	24.1g
Protein	34.7 g
Cholesterol	125 mg
Sodium	1521 mg

* Percent Daily Values are based on a 2,000 calorie diet.

Chili VII

(3 Bean)

(Vegetarian Approved)

Ingredients

- 1 tbsp olive oil
- 1/2 medium onion, diced
- 2 bay leaves
- 1 tsp ground cumin
- 2 tbsps dried oregano
- 1 tbsp salt
- 2 stalks celery, diced
- 2 green bell peppers, diced
- 2 jalapeno peppers, diced
- 3 cloves garlic, diced
- 2 (4 oz.) cans diced green chili peppers, drained
- 2 (12 oz.) packages vegetarian burger crumbles
- 3 (28 oz.) cans whole peeled tomatoes, crushed
- 1/4 C. chili powder

- 1 tbsp ground black pepper
- 1 (15 oz.) can kidney beans, drained
- 1 (15 oz.) can garbanzo beans, drained
- 1 (15 oz.) can black beans
- 1 (15 oz.) can whole kernel corn

Directions

- Stir fry your onions in olive oil then add in: salt, bay leaves, oregano, and cumin, continue frying until the onions become soft then combine in: chili peppers, celery, garlic, bell peppers, garlic, and jalapenos.
- Once everything is hot, about 5 mins of cooking time, add the crumbles.
- Place a lid on the pot, reduce the heating level, and let the contents gently boil for 7 mins.
- Add the tomatoes, beans, pepper, and chili powder.

- Place the lid back on the pot and continue cooking for 50 mins before adding the corn.
- Let the corn cook for 7 mins then shut the heat.
- Let the chili sit for 10 mins before serving.
- Enjoy.

Amount per serving (8 total)

Timing Information:

Preparation	15 m
Cooking	1 h
Total Time	1 h 15 m

Nutritional Information:

Calories	391 kcal
Fat	7.9 g
Carbohydrates	58.7g
Protein	28.2 g
Cholesterol	0 mg
Sodium	2571 mg

* Percent Daily Values are based on a 2,000 calorie diet.

Chili VIII

(Cloves, Allspice, and Cinnamon)

(Ohio Style)

Ingredients

- 1 tbsp vegetable oil
- 1/2 C. diced onion
- 2 lbs ground beef
- 1/4 C. chili powder
- 1 tsp ground cinnamon
- 1 tsp ground cumin
- 1/4 tsp ground allspice
- 1/4 tsp ground cloves
- 1 bay leaf
- 1/2 (1 oz.) square unsweetened chocolate
- 2 (10.5 oz.) cans beef broth
- 1 (15 oz.) can tomato sauce
- 2 tbsps cider vinegar
- 1/4 tsp ground cayenne pepper

- 1/4 C. shredded Cheddar cheese

Directions

- Stir fry your onions for 7 mins, in oil, then add in your beef and stir fry it while crumbling.
- Season the meat with the following: red pepper, chili powder, vinegar, cinnamon, tomato sauce, cumin, broth, allspice, chocolate, cloves, and bay leaf.
- Get everything boiling then place a lid on the pot, and let the contents gently boil for 90 mins stir the chili every 10 mins.
- Place everything the fridge for 8 hrs then heat it back up before serving it all over the pasta.
- Enjoy.

Amount per serving (8 total)

Timing Information:

Preparation	10 m
Cooking	8 h 20 m
Total Time	8 h 30 m

Nutritional Information:

Calories	427 kcal
Fat	35 g
Carbohydrates	7g
Protein	22.2 g
Cholesterol	100 mg
Sodium	659 mg

* Percent Daily Values are based on a 2,000 calorie diet.

Chili IX

(Pork, Salsa, and Beans)

Ingredients

- 1 1/2 lbs pork tenderloin, cut into 2 inch strips
- 1 small onion, coarsely diced
- 1 small red bell pepper, coarsely diced
- 3 (15 oz.) cans black beans
- 1 (16 oz.) jar salsa
- 1/2 C. chicken broth
- 1 tsp dried oregano
- 1 tsp ground cumin
- 2 tsps chili powder

Directions

- Add the following to your slow cooker: chili powder, pork, cumin, onions, oregano, red pepper, salsa, broth, and beans.

- Stir everything before cooking it all for 9 hrs on low heat.
- Take out the pork and shred it before placing it back in the mix and serving the chili.
- Enjoy.

Amount per serving (8 total)

Timing Information:

Preparation	10 m
Cooking	10 h
Total Time	10 h 10 m

Nutritional Information:

Calories	245 kcal
Fat	2.8 g
Carbohydrates	31.9g
Protein	24 g
Cholesterol	37 mg
Sodium	1045 mg

* Percent Daily Values are based on a 2,000 calorie diet.

Chili X

(White Beans)

Ingredients

- 1 tbsp vegetable oil
- 1 onion, diced
- 3 cloves garlic, crushed
- 1 (4 oz.) can diced jalapeno peppers
- 1 (4 oz.) can diced green chili peppers
- 2 tsps ground cumin
- 1 tsp dried oregano
- 1 tsp ground cayenne pepper
- 2 (14.5 oz.) cans chicken broth
- 3 C. diced cooked chicken breast
- 3 (15 oz.) cans white beans
- 1 C. shredded Monterey Jack cheese

Directions

- Stir fry your onions until soft, in oil, then add in, cayenne, garlic, oregano, jalapenos, cumin, and chili peppers.
- Cook this mix for 4 more mins then pour in the beans, chicken, and broth.
- Get everything boiling then set the heat to low and simmer the contents for 17 mins.
- Stir the chili every 4 mins.
- Shut the heat and add the cheese.
- Once the cheese has melted, your chili is ready to serve.
- Enjoy.

Amount per serving (4 total)

Timing Information:

Preparation	10 m
Cooking	20 m
Total Time	30 m

Nutritional Information:

Calories	684 kcal
Fat	16.8 g
Carbohydrates	74.9g
Protein	59.1 g
Cholesterol	1102 mg
Sodium	1896 mg

* Percent Daily Values are based on a 2,000 calorie diet.

Chili XI

(Maggie's Easy Style)

Ingredients

- 2 lbs lean ground beef
- 1 (46 fluid oz.) can tomato juice
- 1 (29 oz.) can tomato sauce
- 1 1/2 C. diced onion
- 1/2 C. diced celery
- 1/4 C. diced green bell pepper
- 1/4 C. chili powder
- 2 tsps ground cumin
- 1 1/2 tsps garlic powder
- 1 tsp salt
- 1/2 tsp ground black pepper
- 1/2 tsp dried oregano
- 1/2 tsp white sugar
- 1/8 tsp ground cayenne pepper
- 2 C. canned red beans, drained and rinsed

Directions

- Stir fry your beef until it is fully done then break it into pieces and remove all excess oils before adding in every ingredient listed.
- Once you have added everything, get the contents boiling.
- Now place a lid on the pot and reduce the heat to low.
- Let the contents gently boil for 90 mins.
- Once the chili has finished let it sit for 30 mins before serving.
- Enjoy.

Amount per serving (10 total)

Timing Information:

Preparation	15 m
Cooking	1 h 30 m
Total Time	1 h 45 m

Nutritional Information:

Calories	347 kcal
Fat	19.9 g
Carbohydrates	22.6g
Protein	21.4 g
Cholesterol	68 mg
Sodium	1246 mg

* Percent Daily Values are based on a 2,000 calorie diet.

Chili XII

(White Beans and Tomatillos)

Ingredients

- 2 tbsps vegetable oil
- 1 onion, diced
- 2 cloves garlic, minced
- 1 (14.5 oz.) can chicken broth
- 1 (18.75 oz.) can tomatillos, drained and diced
- 1 (16 oz.) can diced tomatoes
- 1 (7 oz.) can diced green chilis
- 1/2 tsp dried oregano
- 1/2 tsp ground coriander seed
- 1/4 tsp ground cumin
- 2 ears fresh corn
- 1 lb diced, cooked chicken meat
- 1 (15 oz.) can white beans
- 1 pinch salt and black pepper to taste

Directions

- Stir fry your garlic and onions in oil for about 7 mins until they are tender then add in: spices, broth, chilies and tomatillos, and the tomatoes.
- Get the mix boiling and then lower the height to a light boil.
- Let the mix gently boil for 12 mins. Then add in: beans, chicken and corn.
- Continue cooking for 10 more mins.
- Add in your preferred amount of pepper and salt and then let the chili cool before serving.
- Enjoy.

Amount per serving (9 total)

Timing Information:

Preparation	10 m
Cooking	25 m
Total Time	35 m

Nutritional Information:

Calories	220 kcal
Fat	6.1 g
Carbohydrates	21.2g
Protein	20.1 g
Cholesterol	40 mg
Sodium	786 mg

* Percent Daily Values are based on a 2,000 calorie diet.

Chili XIII

(Black Bean and Basil)

Ingredients

- 1 tbsp vegetable oil
- 1 onion, diced
- 2 cloves garlic, minced
- 1 lb ground turkey
- 3 (15 oz.) cans black beans, undrained
- 2 tbsps ketchup
- 1 (14.5 oz.) can crushed tomatoes
- 1 1/2 tbsps chili powder
- 1 tbsp dried oregano
- 1 tbsp dried basil leaves
- 1 tbsp red wine vinegar

Directions

- Stir fry your garlic and onions until they are see-through then combine in the turkey.

- Continue stir frying until the turkey is evenly browned.
- Now add: vinegar, chili powder, tomatoes, ketchup, basil, beans, and oregano.
- Get everything boiling and then once it is, place a lid on the pot, and set the heat to a low level.
- Cook the mix for 70 mins then stir the contents for 1 min.
- Let the chili sit for 30 mins before serving.
- Enjoy.

Amount per serving (6 total)

Timing Information:

Preparation	20 m
Cooking	1 h 15 m
Total Time	1 h 35 m

Nutritional Information:

Calories	366 kcal
Fat	9.2 g
Carbohydrates	44.1g
Protein	29.6 g
Cholesterol	56 mg
Sodium	969 mg

* Percent Daily Values are based on a 2,000 calorie diet.

Chili XIV

(White Beans and Turkey)

Ingredients

- 1 onion, diced
- 3 cloves garlic, minced
- 1 1/2 lbs ground turkey
- 2 (4 oz.) cans canned green chili peppers, diced
- 1 tbsp ground cumin
- 1 tbsp dried oregano
- 1 tsp ground cinnamon
- ground cayenne pepper to taste
- ground white pepper to taste
- 3 (15 oz.) cans cannellini beans
- 5 C. chicken broth
- 2 C. shredded Monterey Jack cheese

Directions

- Blend one can of your beans in a food processor or blender. Then place the mix in a bowl, to the side.
- Stir fry your turkey, garlic, and onions for 12 mins. Now combine in: cayenne, peppers, white pepper, cinnamon, cumin, and oregano.
- Continue stir frying for 7 more mins.
- Pour in your cans of beans, the puree, and the broth.
- Now add in your cheese and cook for 12 mins before serving hot.
- Enjoy.

Amount per serving (8 total)

Timing Information:

Preparation	15 m
Cooking	30 m
Total Time	45 m

Nutritional Information:

Calories	396 kcal
Fat	17.3 g
Carbohydrates	26.7g
Protein	31.5 g
Cholesterol	92 mg
Sodium	1366 mg

* Percent Daily Values are based on a 2,000 calorie diet.

Chili XV

(Crock Pot I)

Ingredients

- 1 lb ground beef
- 3/4 C. diced onion
- 3/4 C. diced celery
- 3/4 C. diced green bell pepper
- 2 cloves garlic, minced
- 2 (10.75 oz.) cans tomato puree
- 1 (15 oz.) can kidney beans with liquid
- 1 (15 oz.) can kidney beans, drained
- 3 tbsps brown sugar
- 1 (15 oz.) can cannellini beans with liquid
- 1/2 tbsp chili powder
- 1/2 tsp dried parsley
- half jalapeno, diced
- 1 tsp salt
- 3/4 tsp dried basil
- 3/4 tsp dried oregano

- 1/4 tsp ground black pepper
- 1/8 tsp hot pepper sauce

Directions

- Stir fry your beef and then drain the excess oil.
- Add the beef to the crock pot as well as the: beans, jalapenos, tomato puree, onions, garlic, sugar, bell peppers, and celery.
- Add the following as well: hot sauce, chili powder, black pepper, parsley, oregano, salt, basil.
- Place a lid on the slow cooker and cook for 9 hrs with a low level of heat.
- Enjoy.

Amount per serving (8 total)

Timing Information:

Preparation	15 m
Cooking	8 h
Total Time	8 h 15 m

Nutritional Information:

Calories	273 kcal
Fat	7.6 g
Carbohydrates	33.4g
Protein	18.9 g
Cholesterol	34 mg
Sodium	975 mg

* Percent Daily Values are based on a 2,000 calorie diet.

CHILI XVI

(3 BEAN II)

(VEGETARIAN APPROVED)

Ingredients

- 1 (19 oz.) can black bean soup
- 1 (15 oz.) can kidney beans, rinsed and drained
- 1 (15 oz.) can garbanzo beans, rinsed and drained
- 1 (16 oz.) can vegetarian baked beans
- 1 (14.5 oz.) can diced tomatoes in puree
- 1 (15 oz.) can whole kernel corn, drained
- 1 onion, diced
- 1 green bell pepper, diced
- 2 stalks celery, diced
- 2 cloves garlic, diced
- 1 tbsp chili powder, or to taste
- 1 tbsp dried parsley

- 1 tbsp dried oregano
- 1 tbsp dried basil

Directions

- Add the following to your crock pot: garlic, chili powder, celery, parsley, soup, oregano, bell peppers, basil, kidney beans, onions, garbanzos, onions, baked beans, corn, and tomatoes.
- Set the slow cooker to high and cook for 3 hours.
- Let the chili sit for 20 mins before serving.
- Enjoy with a dollop of sour cream.

Amount per serving (8 total)

Timing Information:

Preparation	10 m
Cooking	2 h
Total Time	2 h 10 m

Nutritional Information:

Calories	260 kcal
Fat	2 g
Carbohydrates	52.6g
Protein	12.4 g
Cholesterol	1 mg
Sodium	966 mg

* Percent Daily Values are based on a 2,000 calorie diet.

Chili XVII

(North Carolina Style)

Ingredients

- 2 1/2 lbs ground beef
- 3 stalks celery, diced
- 2 large onions, diced
- 2 cloves garlic, minced
- 1 (29 oz.) can tomato sauce
- 1 (28 oz.) can crushed tomatoes
- 1 (6 oz.) can mushrooms, drained
- 1 1/2 C. dark beer
- 2 (16 oz.) cans chili beans, drained
- 1 (15 oz.) can kidney beans, drained
- 1 tbsp ground cumin
- 1/4 C. chili powder
- 2 tsps ground coriander
- 2 tsps cayenne pepper
- 1 dash Worcestershire sauce

Directions

- Stir fry your beef, in a saucepan, until fully done, and then place it to the side.
- In the drippings fry your onions, garlic, and celery until the onions are see through.
- Then add the beef back into the mix as well as the: Worcestershire, tomatoes and sauce, cayenne, mushrooms, coriander, beer, chili powder, chili beans, cumin, and kidney beans.
- Get everything boiling then lower the heating to medium-low. Cook for 3.5 hours. Stir the chili every 30 mins.
- Enjoy.

Amount per serving (12 total)

Timing Information:

Preparation	15 m
Cooking	3 h 20 m
Total Time	3 h 35 m

Nutritional Information:

Calories	389 kcal
Fat	18.1 g
Carbohydrates	34g
Protein	25.7 g
Cholesterol	57 mg
Sodium	1001 mg

* Percent Daily Values are based on a 2,000 calorie diet.

Chili XVIII

(Quinoa and Cilantro)

Ingredients

- 1 C. uncooked quinoa, rinsed
- 2 C. water
- 1 tbsp vegetable oil
- 1 onion, diced
- 4 cloves garlic, diced
- 1 tbsp chili powder
- 1 tbsp ground cumin
- 1 (28 oz.) can crushed tomatoes
- 2 (19 oz.) cans black beans, rinsed and drained
- 1 green bell pepper, diced
- 1 red bell pepper, diced
- 1 zucchini, diced
- 1 jalapeno pepper, seeded and minced
- 1 tbsp minced chipotle peppers in adobo sauce
- 1 tsp dried oregano

- salt and ground black pepper to taste
- 1 C. frozen corn
- 1/4 C. diced fresh cilantro

Directions

- Boil your quinoa in water for 2 mins before placing a lid on the pot, setting the heat to low, and letting the quinoa cook for 17 mins.
- Stir the quinoa once it has cooled off.
- At the same time, stir fry the onions for 7 mins, in veggie oil, and then add in the cumin, garlic, and chili powder.
- Cook this mix for 2 more mins then add: oregano, tomatoes, chipotles, beans, jalapenos, bell peppers, and zucchini.
- Stir the contents before adding your preferred amount of pepper and salt.

- Get everything boiling and then place a lid on the pot.
- Let the contents gently boil over low heat for 22 mins then add in the corn and quinoa.
- Continue simmering for 7 more mins before adding cilantro.
- Enjoy.

Amount per serving (10 total)

Timing Information:

Preparation	30 m
Cooking	30 m
Total Time	1 h

Nutritional Information:

Calories	233 kcal
Fat	3.5 g
Carbohydrates	42g
Protein	11.5 g
Cholesterol	0 mg
Sodium	540 mg

* Percent Daily Values are based on a 2,000 calorie diet.

Chili XIX

(Apricots and Raisins)

Ingredients

- 1 lb ground beef
- 1 onion, diced
- 1 (14.5 oz.) can stewed tomatoes
- 1 (15 oz.) can tomato sauce
- 1 (15 oz.) can kidney beans
- 1 C. raisins
- 1 C. dried apricots
- 1 1/2 C. water
- 1 pinch chili powder
- 1 pinch garlic powder
- salt and pepper to taste

Directions

- Stir fry your onions and beef until the beef is fully done and the onions are soft.

- Now combine in your tomato sauce, tomato juice, water, black pepper, chili powder, raisins, apricots, garlic powder, and beans.
- Get everything boiling and then place a lid on the pot and gently cook the contents with a low heat for 20 mins.
- Enjoy.

Amount per serving (6 total)

Timing Information:

Preparation	10 m
Cooking	20 m
Total Time	30 m

Nutritional Information:

Calories	394 kcal
Fat	9.2 g
Carbohydrates	48.8g
Protein	30.6 g
Cholesterol	46 mg
Sodium	526 mg

* Percent Daily Values are based on a 2,000 calorie diet.

Chili XX

(Autumn)

Ingredients

- 2 lbs ground beef
- 1 large onion, diced
- 1 green bell pepper, diced
- 2 (15 oz.) cans kidney beans, drained
- 1 (46 fluid oz.) can tomato juice
- 1 (28 oz.) can peeled and diced tomatoes with juice
- 1/2 C. canned pumpkin puree
- 1 tbsp pumpkin pie spice
- 1 tbsp chili powder
- 1/4 C. white sugar

Directions

- Stir fry the beef until fully done then place the meat to the side.

- Now fry your bell pepper and onions in the drippings for 7 mins and then add in: pumpkin, beans, diced tomatoes, and tomato juice.
- Cook for 2 mins before adding in sugar, pumpkin spice, and chili powder.
- Let the contents gently boil with a medium to low level of heat for 90 mins.
- Enjoy.

Amount per serving (8 total)

Timing Information:

Preparation	20 m
Cooking	1 h
Total Time	1 h 20 m

Nutritional Information:

Calories	409 kcal
Fat	16.4 g
Carbohydrates	37.6g
Protein	28.2 g
Cholesterol	69 mg
Sodium	924 mg

* Percent Daily Values are based on a 2,000 calorie diet.

CHILI XXI

(TEXAS STYLE)

Ingredients

- 2 tsps cooking oil
- 3 lbs beef top sirloin, thinly sliced
- 2 lbs sweet Italian sausage, casings removed
- 1 onion, diced
- 1 green bell pepper, diced
- 1 red bell pepper, diced
- 1 yellow bell pepper, diced
- 2 cloves garlic, minced
- 20 oz. diced tomatoes
- 3 (8 oz.) cans tomato sauce
- 2 tsps chicken bouillon granules
- 1/2 C. honey
- 1 (15 oz.) can kidney beans, rinsed and drained
- 2 tbsps cayenne pepper
- 6 tbsps chili powder
- 3 tbsps dried oregano
- 1 tsp ground black pepper

- 2 tsps salt
- 1/3 C. white sugar
- 1 C. shredded Cheddar cheese
- 1/4 C. masa (corn flour)

Directions

- For 7 mins, stir fry the following: garlic, steak, bell peppers, sausage, and onions.
- Now combine in: beans, diced tomatoes, honey, tomato sauce, and bouillon.
- Get everything boiling and then add: sugar, cayenne, salt, chili powder, black pepper, and oregano.
- Let this cook for 2.5 hours before adding your cheese and cooking the mix for another 10 mins until the cheese has melted.
- Simmer the chili with a low heat during this time.
- Add in your flour and cook for 5 more mins.

- Let the chili sit for 10 mins before serving.
- Enjoy.

Amount per serving (12 total)

Timing Information:

Preparation	30 m
Cooking	2 h 15 m
Total Time	2 h 45 m

Nutritional Information:

Calories	675 kcal
Fat	37 g
Carbohydrates	37.6g
Protein	48.3 g
Cholesterol	142 mg
Sodium	1695 mg

* Percent Daily Values are based on a 2,000 calorie diet.

Chili XXII

(3 Pepper)

(Jalapenos, Habaneros, and Anaheim)

Ingredients

- 1/2 lb bacon
- 1 lb ground round
- 1 lb ground pork
- 1 green bell pepper, diced
- 1 yellow onion, diced
- 6 jalapeno peppers, seeded and diced
- 6 habanero peppers, seeded and diced
- 8 Anaheim peppers, seeded and diced
- 2 cloves garlic, minced
- 1 1/2 tbsps ground cumin
- 1 tbsp crushed red pepper flakes
- 3 tbsps chili powder

- 2 tbsps beef bouillon granules
- 1 (28 oz.) can crushed tomatoes
- 2 (16 oz.) cans whole peeled tomatoes, drained
- 2 (16 oz.) cans chili beans, drained
- 1 (12 fluid oz.) can beer
- 3 oz. tomato paste
- 1 oz. chili paste
- 2 C. water

Directions

- Fry your bacon then place it to the side after crumbling it.
- In the same pot, stir fry your pork and beef until fully done then add in: water, garlic, chili paste, cumin, tomato paste, red pepper, beer, chili powder, whole tomatoes, bouillon, and crushed tomatoes.
- Get the mix boiling, reduce the heat, and cook for 55 mins.

- Stir the chili every 5 mins then add the bacon and beans and cook for 20 more mins.
- Let the chili cool off before serving.
- Enjoy.

Amount per serving (8 total)

Timing Information:

Preparation	30 m
Cooking	1 h 30 m
Total Time	2 h

Nutritional Information:

Calories	595 kcal
Fat	31.9 g
Carbohydrates	47.9g
Protein	34.9 g
Cholesterol	91 mg
Sodium	1575 mg

* Percent Daily Values are based on a 2,000 calorie diet.

Chili XXIII

(Cannellini and Cheddar)

Ingredients

- 2 1/2 lbs lean ground beef
- salt to taste
- 1 medium onion, diced
- 1 green bell pepper, seeded and diced (optional)
- 3 cloves garlic, pressed
- 1/4 C. Worcestershire sauce
- 5 tbsps chili powder
- 2 tsps ground cumin
- 2 tsps dried oregano
- 1 (15 oz.) can kidney beans, rinsed and drained
- 1 (15 oz.) can cannellini beans, rinsed and drained
- 2 (12 oz.) bottles chili sauce
- 1 (14 oz.) can beef broth
- 2 C. shredded Cheddar cheese
- 1/4 C. diced jalapeno pepper (optional)

Directions

- Stir fry your beef then add in the garlic, bell peppers, and onions.
- Cook the mix for 5 mins and then add: oregano, Worcestershire, cumin, and chili powder.
- Let the contents cook for 7 more mins then add: beans, broth, and chili sauce.
- Place a lid on the pot and let it gently boil with a low level of heat for 40 mins.
- When serving the chili add a garnishing of jalapenos and cheddar.
- Enjoy.

Amount per serving (6 total)

Timing Information:

Preparation	15 m
Cooking	50 m
Total Time	1 h 5 m

Nutritional Information:

Calories	900 kcal
Fat	56.4 g
Carbohydrates	40.8g
Protein	56.9 g
Cholesterol	1190 mg
Sodium	1109 mg

* Percent Daily Values are based on a 2,000 calorie diet.

Chili XXIV

(Roman Style)

Ingredients

- 1 lb lean ground beef
- 3/4 C. diced onion
- 1 (26 oz.) jar three cheese spaghetti sauce
- 1 1/2 C. water
- 2 tsps sugar
- 1 (14.5 oz.) can diced tomatoes
- 1 (4 oz.) can sliced mushrooms
- 2 oz. sliced pepperoni
- 1 tbsp beef bouillon
- 1 tbsp chili powder
- 1 (14.5 oz.) can kidney beans, drained and rinsed
- 1 C. shredded Cheddar cheese, for garnish

Directions

- Stir your beef, then cook for your onions, for 7 mins, in the drippings.
- Now add the following to the onions: beans, pasta sauce, chili powder, water, bouillon, sugar, pepperoni, tomatoes, and mushrooms.
- Get the mixture boiling and then lower the heat.
- Let the contents cook for 40 mins.
- Enjoy.

Amount per serving (6 total)

Timing Information:

Preparation	5 m
Cooking	40 m
Total Time	45 m

Nutritional Information:

Calories	489 kcal
Fat	26 g
Carbohydrates	34.5g
Protein	28.3 g
Cholesterol	82 mg
Sodium	1407 mg

* Percent Daily Values are based on a 2,000 calorie diet.

CHILI XXV

(BACKROAD STYLE)

Ingredients

- 1 C. elbow macaroni
- 1 lb ground beef
- 1 small onion, diced
- 1 C. diced celery
- 1/2 large green bell pepper, diced
- 1 (15 oz.) can kidney beans, drained
- 2 (10.75 oz.) cans condensed tomato soup
- 2 (14.5 oz.) cans diced tomatoes
- 1/8 C. brown sugar
- salt and pepper to taste

Directions

- Boil your pasta in water for 9 mins then remove all the liquid.

- Meanwhile boil your green pepper and celery in water for 5 mins then remove the liquid as well.
- Now stir fry your beef until fully done and combine in the onions and cook them until they are see-through.
- Now add in the celery mix, and: brown sugar, kidney beans, and tomato soup.
- Simmer everything for 10 mins then shut the heat and add in some pepper and salt and the pasta.
- Enjoy.

Amount per serving (6 total)

Timing Information:

Preparation	15 m
Cooking	25 m
Total Time	40 m

Nutritional Information:

Calories	489 kcal
Fat	22.4 g
Carbohydrates	49.2g
Protein	22.1 g
Cholesterol	64 mg
Sodium	997 mg

* Percent Daily Values are based on a 2,000 calorie diet.

Thanks for Reading! Now Let's Try some Sushi and Dump Dinners....

Send the Book!

To grab this **box set** simply follow the link mentioned above, or tap the book cover.

This will take you to a page where you can simply enter your email address and a PDF version of the **box set** will be emailed to you.

I hope you are ready for some serious cooking!

[Send the Book!](#)

You will also receive updates about all my new books when they are free.

Also don't forget to like and subscribe on the social networks. I love meeting my readers. Links to all my profiles are below so please click and connect :)

[Facebook](#)

[Twitter](#)

COME ON...
LET'S BE FRIENDS :)

I adore my readers and love connecting with them socially. Please follow the links below so we can connect on Facebook, Twitter, and Google+.

Facebook

Twitter

I also have a blog that I regularly update for my readers so check it out below.

My Blog

Can I Ask A Favour?

If you found this book interesting, or have otherwise found any benefit in it. Then may I ask that you post a review of it on Amazon? Nothing excites me more than new reviews, especially reviews which suggest new topics for writing. I do read all reviews and I always factor feedback into my newer works.

So if you are willing to take ten minutes to write what you sincerely thought about this book then please visit our Amazon page and post your opinions.

Again thank you!

INTERESTED IN OTHER EASY COOKBOOKS?

Everything is easy! Check out my Amazon Author page for more great cookbooks:

For a complete listing of all my books please see my author page.

Made in the USA
Middletown, DE
09 October 2020